CAPTURED THOUGHTS

DISCOVER THE DEEPER MEANING OF LIFE

JERREL E. WOLFE

ISBN
9798218713119 (Paperback)

Captured Thoughts is dedicated to my grandchildren carrying the blood and blessings of a gifted poet. May their lives be as fruitful and blessed as this author. Brynn Baker, Delaney Baker, and Sullivan Malone

TABLE OF CONTENTS

THE POET

Rembrandt painted with the brush.
Mozart struck the keys.
Shakespeare penned the mighty word.
Foundations set by these.

Bits of mighty legends
are found within my prose.
God's gifted me with insight
and the ink that always flows.

I seek to make you ponder,
pause your daily life,
to spend some time with each piece
I write for you tonight.

It may help you with your family,
enlighten you to history past,
Carry you in your darkest moments,
and remember loved ones passed.

Blessed by my creator,
I pass these on to you.
Knowing that from this cup you sip,
my message will come through.

A Poet's Bath

A poet's mind immerses
into a realm of celestial bliss.
Soaking in warm waters,
finding words that need a kiss.

Penning them to parchment
captured for years to come.
Sharing with the world's great readers
those enjoying poetic fun.

The genre is quite unique,
great stories I do tell.
Imparting years of wisdom
with the rhyme of my inkwell.

I'll capture you in deeper thought,
you will relive distant dreams.
Find growth and strength inherent,
enjoying all my themes.

In each peace I'll share my being
I'll touch your heart and soul.
You will wrestle with emotion,
perhaps, find life's destined goal.

There are various poetic perspectives
and future books to print.
All brought forth from the mental bath,
a universe from which they're sent.

Marathon of Life

Each day, our trek moves forward
in the marathon of life.
Contending with the dangers,
the troubles, and the strife.

We may find ourselves running in the pack
and sometimes far behind.
Confidence and energy
are the tools that we must find.

Belief that we can conquer
all that's thrown our way.
Slowly moves us forward,
in a race run day to day.

With heart you must increase your stride
as you see the end is near.
Pride will yield the final burst
as you reach your final year.

You will know that you're a winner
looking back upon your race,
With accolades placed upon you
through His amazing grace.

PUZZLED

I'm puzzled with the life bestowed
upon the troubled mass.
Those searching for a meaning,
a partnership to last.

Life's puzzle does not come in a box
with perfection shown on the cover.
We search through all the pieces,
perhaps finding a needed lover.

Over time the framework forms,
yet the challenge still remains,
to complete the masterpiece of life,
despite your labored pains.

You will find configuration
and seek the proper fit,
trying bits and pieces
just for the hell of it.

When connection does occur,
you feel the pride in this.
Each piece adjoins its soulmate
and fits in perfect bliss.

So, here's a toast to life's puzzle
and the soulmate you must find.
A connection like no other
when all the pieces do align.

POWER OF THE TONGUE

We speak of good and evil.
It surrounds us every day.
We see our morals fading.
Less faith leads us astray.

We speak the Devil's language.
We curse and judge our friends.
Seldom ever giving the thought.
of declining family trends.

When's the last time you gave a blessing
the last time you held a door?
Offered up a thank you
of all things needed to implore?

Start with something simple,
Feel the joy that it brings.
Eradicate the evil speech
and let light shine again.

REFLECTION

As an aging senior citizen,
I reflect on times gone by.
In dreams I relive the memories,
now realize time does fly.

Used to be a time
when a hip joint was in a great place.
But now I try to hide the pain,
sitting silent in this space.

At ten I played in the creek,
I find it now in my neck.
No running, jumping, tumbling.
Life's become quite a wreck.

I find the eyes are failing.
Often feel the need to go.
I dread the feel of winter,
once loved the frozen snow.

So now the joy is grand kids,
A love I've never known.
Their hugs and admiration
fills my life till I'm called home.

BEAUTY

There's beauty in an apple
hanging from the tree.
There's beauty in each and all of us,
sometimes not plain to see.

There's beauty in a thank you,
smiles, touch, and gifts we give.
In this harried world we live in,
it's easily smothered in the life we live.

Can you see the beauty in a book
and the joy of a child to read.
The loving touch of a mother,
sparkling eyes of the child she feeds.

I ask, you think about this message
and the enlightenment it will bring, when you
take the time to realize there's beauty
in most each and everything.

Have you stopped to view the houses
built since a hundred years have passed?
Or marveled at a sunset
where colored clouds amassed?

What about the athlete
or jet trails in the sky?
Beauty is ever present.
It will sometimes make you cry.

Beauty is in the simple things.
Take the time to see.
It's there for you to create and view,
becoming one with harmony.

CRUMBLING ELEGANCE

Everything that comes from Earth
goes back if not maintained.
We often see decay in life.
Things changing, not the same.

So much artistic beauty
and structures built by man.
Falling to the wayside
to the end of its lifespan.

Pause and take a moment
as you live from day to day,
To find appreciation
of things that fade away.

You'll gain a great perspective
of others from past years,
see resolve and character,
before history disappears.

FINDING PEACE

Outside the cottage window
a forest filled with trees.
Pines are gently swaying
amidst the autumn breeze.

I see a whiff of snow flakes
kissing the cottage glass.
A crackle in the fireplace,
cool wine now fills my glass.

I peer down the winding road.
lights flicker in the distance.
I feel the sullen silence
and reflect on my existence.

It's been quite a while
since I've asked the simple question.
Just what is my purpose here,
my destiny, and my mission?

Has my life made a ripple
in Earth's majestic sea?
Have I fulfilled that plan
God has placed inside of me?

Tonight, my soul is restless
as I peer atop the pass.
Gazing at the waning moon,
I see breath upon the glass.

In this, I see a sign of life
that God has granted me.
Content, that I am in His grace,
knowing He'll rescue me.

GUARDIAN'S GRIP

Know that I have been here.
I'm with you every day.
So many times I have reached out
when your life's in disarray.

My grip is everlasting,
I've got you in my hand.
At times you need your inner strength,
dig deep and stake your stand.

It's often I will test you
when roadblocks do amass.
Hold fast and know I would never give you
a test you could not pass.

FINDING HOME

In the distance, the iron horse whistle.
Hoof steps clatter down the street.
Lamplighter lighting up the lights.
Winter biting at my feet.

Another day has come and gone.
Sun has set just to the west.
I'll seek a place of warmth tonight
and sleep as nature's guest.

The war between the blue and grey
has left me without a home.
Family and friends, all been lost.
The city streets I now do roam.

At main streets end I view a church.
Its bell now calls to me.
Flickering shadows through stain glass lights,
faint songs now rescue me.

In songs my mind surrenders.
Beneath trees I sleep tonight.
Knowing God is with me,
providing protection in this fight.

A Teaching
Moment

Today I taught my daughter
how to sit and pray.
She folded up her little hands,
I winked and said, *"Okay!"*

Now close your eyes and picture
a Man who made the stars,
a Man who made the sunshine
and provides your candy bars.

The One who holds your hand
when mommy is not near,
the One who will protect you
when the storms come which you fear.

Now see His smile,
His loving touch,
and know that He's your friend.
We speak with Him each morning
and when each day shall end.

It's now the time we thank Him
for putting food upon your plate.
Providing all your wants and needs,
instilling love, not hate.

Tell Him that you love Him.
Thank Him every day.
We call Him our Lord Jesus
and this is how you pray.

BECOMING A FATHER

We didn't know our destiny
at the age of seventeen.
Life was so exciting
for a maturing teen.

A car and a girlfriend,
great music of the past.
The nights moved by so quickly.
Just hoping they would last.

We made it home by midnight,
chores were done each day.
Engaging in America's sport,
we loved to go and play.

And then a nation to serve
a lady to come home to.
Surprise of a sudden family,
a life I never knew.

Fatherhood was a blessing.
Life changing in many ways.
True bonding with the family,
enjoying all those holidays.

Instilling all I had to give
to the children I loved so much.
Today, the gift returned one hundred fold
in the respect they have for us.

It's great to be a father.
It took work and strong will.
However, without these loved ones in my life,
it would never be fulfilled.

WUV DA WABBIT

Wuv the wittle bunny
for its he you see
That will turn into a Wabbit,
to be our dwelicacy.

Polwish up your shotgun
and put your hunting boots on.
The wabbit's coming va—wee soon
and I have the shell to seal his doom.

I've chased the cwazy wabbits
throught my wifetime.
I never will-we got one
but maybe one this time.

I'll get him in my headwight,
I'll wack 'em wike a mole.
I chase at wittle quitt-a
down that wabbit hole.

He thinks he willlllllllll... outsmart me
but it's pwain to see
That pesky wittle wabbit
won't get the best of me.

THE BAKER

It's 3 am the alarm clock sounds
time to make the donuts.
Trapped in the sugar-filled revolving door
this pace could drive one nuts!

Each day a new fresh pastry,
work the dough, and make the pie.
A dozen here and a dozen there,
another sweet tooth to satisfy.

It takes a special person
to work and toil this way,
repeating over and over the daily grind,
while life just passes away.

The baker doesn't get the tips
and recognition's seldom there,
slaving in the background,
patrons don't seem to care.

So hats off the bakers,
provider of the smile.
The world would be much different
had they chosen another lifestyle.

MADISON'S BLESSING

The Lord will often bless us
in ways we cannot see,
guide us through hard times
and bring us to where we ought to be.

A child of eleven
who sang since the age of four,
sat in a TV audience
with aging father and many more.

When during a commercial break
a mic was passed through the masses,
Just to hear a song or two
from those who hadn't had classes.

First one and then another
and when the break was about to end,
a child was given a chance to sing,
"America's Got Talent" about to begin!

She sang in acapella
her notes rang crisp, no fear.
Judges who were readying,
couldn't help but listen dear.

"Amazing Grace" rang loud and clear that day
as hundreds sat in awe.
Somehow the Lord God our savior
had entered in the hall.

The judges brought her forward
and placed her on the stage.
Asked her why she never auditioned.
She said "Because of age."

They ask to hear it once again
and why she sang so true.
It was because of her belief in God
and a father whose life was nearly through.

Cancer and a financial pinch
was the problem family faced.
Dad was in his final stages,
he needed amazing grace.

When the child had settled in,
prayers touched every ear.
Judges slammed the golden buzzer.
That prayed-for miracle was here.

BLINDSIDED

Yesterday I was important,
today I think not so.
Why did such change come about,
answers I just don't know.

A wise man would have prepared himself
and planned for such as this,
living life alone
without another's kiss.

Life's lesson is now upon me
such a crushing blow,
to know just how important
and then just being left go.

Answers, I don't have them.
It will never be quite clear,
How quickly change can come about in life
and leave you left with fear.

TIME TRAVEL

God's given us a gift
to travel through out time.
To relive precious moments
stored in the corners of your mind.

The past is always present
when you take the time to sit.
Relax into the moment
and pause for just a bit.

Days of joyous pleasure,
friends you once held dear.
Bring smiles to sullen faces
looking back from year to year.

Children growing up so fast.
Decisions you have made.
Relived in the moments,
pondering your life's great parade.

Life is short we've come to know
So take the time for this.
Travel back in time with memories
life's joys to reminisce.

FORGOTTEN RINGS

The rings of matrimony
are now sitting in a drawer.
The beauty of commitment
lost forevermore.

I hold each in my hand tonight
reaching deep to see the why,
that the special love between us
eventually would die.

That special love of twenty
now eroded by thirty-three,
stresses of the workplace,
children with so much need.

And then at forty-five or six
counseling was not the glue.
Nights of quiet desperation
seeking the partner I once knew.

So when the kids have left the house
more emptiness is felt.
Each day I search for happiness
in this life that I've been dealt.

Alone and separated,
I hold one ring in each hand,
looking to the future
and a love that can withstand.

A Restless Night

I dreamed that I went back in time
and traveled through a portal,
when I was just but seventeen,
feeling quite immortal.

Energy was abundant,
future so exciting.
Freedom and love experienced
this new world so inviting.

I saw the many pitfalls
in life I had to deal.
Knew I couldn't change a thing
and wisdom made this real.

Re-experiencing bad decisions
and the troubles on my road.
I wanted to correct them
knowing what I had sewed.

Twas not the case in this restless dream
where I was trapped to live past,
knowing that each step I took
would not be my last.

I couldn't change the history
or problems I had caused,
couldn't correct bad judgment
or fix my many flaws.

In this dream, I relived my lifetime
seeing all the errors I had made.
Awoke in darkened silence
in a bed which now I laid.

Alone and quite remorseful,
I knew I could do better.
Now a new day lies before me.
Each footstep, I will measure.

So Close

Upon my kitchen counter
is a mixer and a blender,
inviting such ingredients
that seldom make us slender.

In the fridge, I find the ice cream
and frozen pizza pie.
So many things to choose from,
all there to catch my eye.

Pop it in the oven.
Prepare to make a shake.
Just about to finish,
the alarm clock makes me wake.

There is no steamy pizza,
no ice cream yet in store.
Just a morning cup of coffee,
off to work and out the door.

THE SKIER

I look up to the mountain,
sun shining at my back.
Riding that first lift chair
I prepare for the powder attack.

Thirteen inches of new snow
had fallen overnight.
I'm now in line to be the first
to ski the fall line with delight.

With goggles now firmly in place
hair tucked 'neath my hat,
Over the crest, I take my place,
God's country is where I'm at.

A swooping left and then a right
pole plants upon feather-light snow.
A serenity glides down with me,
I love this feeling so.

It's me and Mother Nature,
a smoothness never felt.
Sking God's backcountry
with the skill that I've been dealt.

From the bottom of that hill
I look to friends approaching.
Their tracks intersect with mine
in an up-down figure-eight motion.

In front of me, a lake I see
a snowboard skier's town.
A hop turn, and a deep breath,
I ski the rest of the way down.

It's here I see the children,
the families that have come to play.
Upon this snow-covered hillside
on a sunlit wintery day.

There's music in the village.
A bonfire burning through the ground.
Toddies, smiles, and friendly faces,
boarders and skiers all around.

Don't knock it till you've tried it,
this is winter at its best
At most any ski slope in this land
you can pass the NASTAR test.

LOSING MANHOOD

Where's the man who can build it,
the man who can fix it,
the one who can grow it,
hunt it, or catch it?

Where have we come as society
to lose what's made us great?
Relying on a handout
to get what's on our plate.

The pride of work and honor
brought ladies to our door,
Laid foundations for our families,
our wealth, and so much more.

Past time we peel back the onion
and get down to the core,
of what and where we lost it,
in hopes we can restore.

It's not about the money,
it's not about the me.
It's all about faith and trust
and building family.

CATCHING A COMET

Every day I wake restricted,
bound in this chair I sit,
taking journeys in my mind
just for the hell of it.

I've mastered an art while in this space.
I'm not here in total stagnation.
A worldly traveler I've become,
my mind's my inspiration.

Today, as I sit and stare into the rain
attuned to its placid rhythm,
I take another journey
and bless this gift I'm given.

For I've danced in misty rivers,
swung from rainbows in the sky.
Kissed the edge of eternity,
and ran through fields of rye.

I feel life's journey is ending here
as I sit on this final day,
An Angel here is with me
to see me on my way.

She says we'll take a journey,
the two of us this time.
We'll leave this earth behind us,
together we will fly.

We'll catch and ride a comet.
Flash through the blackened night.
Wake up in the morning
and finally stand upright.

I'll talk to God of my journeys
and the two of us shall speak,
for I am bound to Heaven,
leaving my wheelchair with the meek.

A Christmas to Remember

That river road was quiet
at midnight Christmas eve,
when I stopped to view the snowflakes
upon the fallen locust leaves.

Lights flickered in the distance,
there was snow for miles and miles.
I found myself immersed in Christmas
for just a little while.

What gift this is discovered
to hear faint crying in the breeze.
Alone in all reality,
a homeless man brought me to my knees.

His first words "Merry Christmas",
as tears streamed down his face.
I placed my hand upon him
and asked for God's amazing grace.

"Whatever has you troubled
or whatever causes pain,
let's get out of the weather
and find some warmth again!"

I helped him to the carriage,
his body very frail,
offered him a sip of wine
from my holy grail.

He told me of his family,
the children he had lost.
Hard times had fallen on him.
He could not afford the cost.

This Christmas he was crying.
Feelings were all he had.
Emotions of a dying man
had left him oh so sad.

"God is all I have right now,
no home or food or friends.
Thank you for your kindness
and now the story ends".

Hooves clattered up the cobblestone path,
snowflakes more intense,
warmth was now inside the gate
just past the picket fence.

He told me I was his Angel
while I did not think so.
He said, "God had sent me
as it was his time to go.

He offered me a prayer
in a weak and trailing voice
and in his last breath of life imparted....
"When God is all you have
God is all you need"

ANOTHER PASSING

Another friend has come and gone.
I guess they've passed the test.
Today I wrestle with the grief
God has placed upon my nest.

The fear of death has long since past
I know there's Heaven's grace.
Questions of "How I live this life?"
now smacks me in the face.

I know God has a plan for me.
"Have I fulfilled my task?"
Looking towards tomorrow
in His direction, I will ask.

You see it's very simple
to walk with God each day.
Ask for grace and mercy.
Seek His direction when you pray.

With that said,
enjoy your day as you walk upon this land.
Know that eternal life awaits you,
And your fate is within God's hand.

CHERISH THE KISS

Today I write a piece for you
and send it on its way,
hoping to touch a piece of you
in your life of disarray.

Do you often ponder why you're here,
in this life you've come to know,
and look back on your earthly path
and the seeds that you did sow?

Do you take the time to enjoy the stars,
the trees, and the autumn leaves,
relish the warmth of sunshine
and the coolness of a breeze?

Have you taken time for God this week
and given Him just a minute,
or stressed about life's ups and downs asking
why you're trapped up in it.

There's beauty all around you
and God has placed you here.
Have you thought about your mission
or opened up your ear?

The Lord God often speaks to you
despite times you seldom pray.
He knows your wants and needs and more
and walks with you every day.

He is there when you sip that coffee,
there when raindrops kiss your sleeve.
Walking alongside you,
he is your daily reprieve.

Take this time to know this,
to seek out heavenly bliss,
for you are a child of God,
blessed daily with His kiss.

FINAL THOUGHTS

Today I've had a thousand thoughts.
My final day has come.
I've walked the Earth and spent a life
from this end, I cannot run.

Regrets there are many,
there's still sorrow in my heart.
I've asked the Lord for blessings,
and grace before I depart.

Great memories of a childhood,
destruction of past wars,
lost friends, and family members,
perhaps I'll see again, once more.

It all moved by so quickly.
Time would not stand still.
Years just not remembered,
enjoying my free will.

Know we all will reach this place
when the time comes to an end,
precious minutes to capture and recollect
before our soul transcends.

The clicking of the stopwatch
mirrors the beating of the heart,
continually unwinding,
until the day that we depart.

ANGELS DON'T WRINKLE

Angels don't wrinkle.
Angels don't creak.
Angels don't ache or pain
or have a restless night's sleep.

Another Angel has earned her wings
following in God's path,
traveling in the Lord's footprints,
performing deeds and tasks.

Risen into a new life,
no pain or misery.
She will be with you in a sunrise
and delivering prayers from a bended knee.

Another Angel is among us,
guarding and protecting our path.
Angels don't wrinkle,
just radiate their Heavenly craft.

ANGELIC RECOLLECTION

Learning to live,
learning to love,
learning the values
instilled from above.

Today I live at the right hand of God,
building another home,
preparing for my family
with the seeds that I have sewn.

My journey, sometimes arduous.
My life, a work of art.
I've planted seeds of love and faith
and I leave one loving thought.

It's only love that sets us free
from this world and all its strife,
and it's God's grace and mercy
that through His child, I have a new life.

FAITH HEALS

Driving down I-95,
all possessions in the van,
caught up in depression,
doing the best I can.

Life's crushing blows had struck me.
So much pain in all of this,
to lose a child of seven,
never more to kiss.

A crash and seventy would end this
but the van began to slow,
coming to rest by the underpass
lit by a faint dim glow.

It was there the Lord reached out to me.
I saw Him on the cross.
Viewed His pain and agony
and felt what He had lost.

I heard Him whisper to my soul,
"Keep faith, you're in my hand,
Your daughter here is with Me,
it's all part of My plan."

"When you have completed My journey
and eternal life begins,
she'll be waiting for you
along with all your friends."

FULFILLING DIRECTION

Again, I ask the question
as to why I've been placed here.
Seven decades passing,
and the reason is still not clear.

Have I fulfilled my mission?
Has God still a plan,
to use this mortal vessel
as an agent of His hand?

It's something to be wrestled with
as we've been placed here for a reason,
enjoying all the fruits of life
from season to coming season.

So as the sun breaks over the mountain,
coffee now in hand,
I ask again for direction,
believing in God's greater plan.

APPRECIATION

So there I was,
atop the mountain I always wished to climb.
Looking down upon the beauty
that my footsteps left behind.

The trek required some effort,
the aging legs feel pain.
All is overshadowed
with the view from this domain.

I'm one step closer to Heaven.
There's a freshness in the air.
In the peaceful joy of nature,
I've lost all my despair.

For it's here I see my blessings
in a life lived far from grace.
Appreciation for creation,
I await His sweet embrace.

JOY AND MAGIC

Another day is upon us.
We walk our daily path.
Not knowing what the future is,
we are products of our past.

In this world we live in
some things may not be seen.
Joy and magic coming together,
to make the angels sing.

There's joy and magic in a sunrise
peeking through the trees.
Joy and magic in the fireworks
on celebrations eve.

There's joy and magic in a birth
and when your power ball is drawn.
So many times you'll miss it
each and every dawn.

I am blessed to see in this lifetime
the paralyzed rise to walk.
Imminent death confronted
and healing from the frock.

There's joy in walking with our God
and magic in His grace.
Let these lifetime joys.
Keep smiles upon your face.

IT'S A LINEAR WORLD

There are headlines and timelines,
sidelines and fault lines,
coastlines deadlines,
goal and guidelines.

You may find a receding hairline,
Borderline, storyline, chorus line,
waterline, bloodline.
Perhaps, get to the front of the line.

From production line to transmission line,
we all will walk the line,
and when we reach the finish line,
shall await God's call on the hotline.

PLANTING THE GARDEN

What have you planted in your garden?
Have you prepped the soil?
Have you thought about the seeds amassed,
your work and life so toiled?

Realizing each seed has a season,
which one needs planting first?
The welcomed harvest of your work
will give your life rebirth.

So first love must be planted
for from it, the Earth is blessed.
A good yield of stability
will help withstand this earthly test.

An acre of assurance
will fill your field with confidence.
This garden of your soul will survive
without the need of a fence.

Ethics will provide the vitamins
to make your morals strong,
giving you the mental strength,
to know what's right from wrong.

Before the sun does set this day,
on the garden you have sown,
plant a row of compassion,
closest to your home.

Your harvest will be plentiful
and each day your soul shall feed,
nurtured by your garden
and the virtue of your creed.

FIRST BREATH

Today a soul has found a home
in the newness of a birth.
Breathing life into a tiny child
who inherits God's created Earth.

This child will taste the goodness
of all God has in store,
walk in the path of achievements
ancestors laid down at the door.

With love and adoration
parents will lead the way.
A journey to adulthood,
maturing day to day.

Upon that graduation
when soul and child are free,
their marriage will paint a picture
of what we call history.

TRIBUTE TO MOTHERS

The voice within me yearns to speak,
to take the pen in hand.
Bring to light "MOTHERHOOD"
to all who walk this land.

God gave this gift to women
entrusting them the chore,
to carry His creation
for now and ever more.

He granted them the patience,
the unconditional love,
to mold and hold and nurture
this gift from up above.

Chosen to be the anchor,
known to be the glue,
to mend life's shattered pieces,
ensuring they get through.

Hopes and dreams will be shelved.
She'll live through good days and bad.
Placing all upon her shoulders,
should children lose their dad.

A mother and educator,
a nurse, chauffer, and a cook.
Birth-to-death dedication,
not found in any book.

BROKEN VOWS

Love left the perfect marriage
of two who became one,
sacred vows of matrimony
have now become undone.

Never was I ready for
or prepared for this day,
that a soulmate I thought I found
would up and walk away.

You won't see me wear this picture,
I'll smile despite my fear,
I'll live this life appearing stronger
than the feeling I hold dear.

Living now with love left behind,
nightly traveling down the memory lane,
knowing that all hopes and dreams
will never be the same.

Questions, there are many.
Answers may not be found,
as to why once everlasting love
gets trampled to the ground.

LOVE'S PRICE

It is said that everything has a price,
a sum that we must pay.
Love is no exception,
bestowed along our way.

It's given out on credit.
We cherish it so much,
never giving a thought to the price,
or how it affects us.

Love will pull your purse strings.
The price can be quite dear.
Grief that can come with it
could last from year to year.

Not to shy away from,
accept it when it comes.
Know that if you lose it,
your life may come undone.

ARLINGTON

I heard the faint sound of taps
at Arlington that day,
and viewed the granite headstones
of so many gone away.

I traveled back
within my mind, to 1864,
to view the many caissons
carrying those of civil war.

The fathers and the sons,
the lives that had been lost,
embracing all the freedoms,
ultimate death to be the cost.

In the waning sunlight
at Arlington that day,
I dropped down to one knee
and felt the need to pray.

I had glanced at many
markers from 1864
1917, forty-one, sixty seven,
and 1994.

If I viewed one hundred thousand,
there would be many more to see,
because this is what it took
to keep a nation free.

I see Timothy and Richard, Jack,
John, and Jim,
sacrificing their all
for they knew they had to win.

The cracking sounds of a gun salute
brought me back from my sullen trance.
I wipe the tears from my eyes
and took an upright stance.

I snapped up to attention
and the right hand swung around.
This salute came from the heart
to honor those in hallowed ground.

SENT TO WAR

They gave us a big story
of why we went to war,
drafted and enlisted us
changed lives forevermore.

With gun in hand we took our stand,
dropped on foreign shore.
So many brothers' lives were lost,
death always at the door.

Snipers and the jungle,
rice paddies and the tunnel.
Weapons we relied upon
sometimes not quite functional.

Called upon and duty done,
it was back to our hometown,
with little appreciation
for those who wore the Vietnam crown.

JOURNEY OF LOVE

The love of sixteen
was extra special at best.
The beauty in the eyes,
heart thumping in the chest.

Butterflies and laughter
filled up each day,
awaiting the moment
the two of us could play.

At forty it's quite different,
so many things we've learned,
struggling with life's issues,
so many times been burned.

But though all the hard times
we've built a legacy.
A nice home with two children,
in respected love, we've found the key.

At sixty, the love of Grandchildren
adds to the love of you and me.
Our bodies feeling the age and time
as we approach our destiny.

It's here we find our love
in just a simple touch.
Seeing so much more inside
than bodies that have aged so much.

Beauty is now found in the soul
and not upon the surface.
Sensuality- the subtle look- and kindness
really shows its purpose.

Love is everchanging.
It's not from the eyes in which you see.
It's ultimately in the heart
that joins us in harmony.

REFLECTION

As an aging senior citizen,
I reflect on times gone by.
In dreams, I relive the memories
and realize time does fly.

Used to be a time
when a hip joint was a great place.
Now I try to hide the pain
sitting silent in this space.

At ten, I played in the creek
I find it now in my neck.
No running, jumping, tumbling,
life's become quite a wreck!

I find the eyes are failing,
often feel the need to go.
I dread the feel of winter,
once loved the frozen snow.

So now the joy is "grandkids",
a love I've never known.
Their hugs and admiration
fills my life till I'm called home.

THE HOMESTEAD

Most trees are gone, the view has changed
of a scene sixty years since past.
Grandparents now departed,
their history now to last.

The siding a bit more weathered,
so much rearranged,
the fence and shutters missing.
Mind's caught up in this change.

There's a treasure in one last standing oak
I climbed when just a kid.
The lawn tool shed now missing
where I often hid.

Six hundred miles to take this trip
just to see and reminisce,
changes over decades,
vision, past family I do miss.

It was just a needed visit.
Captured memories came to life.
When I relived my history
with grandchildren and my wife.

REMEMBERING JOHN HARPER

The night the Titanic went down,
1500-plus people were destined to drown.

A preacher John Harper was searching to find
the many lost souls, tossed in the brine.

Swimming to many, seeking to save young and old,
all the lost sinners not in the fold.

While clinging to the debris a man calmly said, "No"
John's pleas were not accepted so his life jacket did go.

"You need this more than I young man!"
Swimming off to do all he can.

Saving lost souls in the dead of night,
such a losing battle amidst all the fright.

Minutes later John came back to the man,
helped him to a lifeboat, extended his hand.

Freezing, and when all energy spent
that gallant preacher was Heaven-sent.

Now back on dry land survivors amassed
to speak of the night loved ones slipped from their grasp.

And then on the podium, four years had gone
by for those pulled from the sea.

Questions lingering of what happened and why
and how this all came to be.

Now led to Christ tears streamed from the man,
pulled from the sea by God's saving hand.

With tears in his eyes the night he spoke,
he recalled John Harper's drowning heroic quote.

Believe in the name of the Lord
and you will be Heaven-sent.

JIMMY BUFFET

I find my heart is heavy,
bad news has hit my ear,
that singer, songwriter Jimmy Buffet
is no longer here.

There will be no more wasting away
in a place called Margaritaville.
For he has hopped to Pleasure Island
where the drinks are always filled.

Cheeseburgers will be much better,
Latitude of life no longer charted.
Temptations of this Earthly world
will be no longer bartered.

He's found his five O'clock amongst the clouds,
no longer wondering where.
And San Francisco was not his destination
for this Labor Day weekend fair.

Hush puppies on and drink in hand.
Come Monday everything will be alright.
For the greatest icon of island music
has just been released from indenture,
Having taken his final fight.

A MOTHER'S SON

"Morning Dove" a name long lost
in American History.
Born on the open plains
named by the Cherokee.

It was the 1800s,
native species were not blessed.
Exploited by the settlers
armies moved them from their nest.

Survival was not certain,
treaties were not kept.
Families were not for certain,
thousands of tears were wept.

Morning Dove survivedthe strife
through wars and troubled times.
Leading children into a 20th century,
surviving all past crimes.

Then as the time did pass
heritage was passed down.
The rise of a new found nation
created many towns.

Down in Mississippi
in a place called Tupelo,
a great great grandson came to life
in a man we've all come to know...
Elvis Presley

HOLD ON TO YOUR HAPPY FACE

When anger fills the moment,
clear thoughts cannot come through,
lasered on annoying things
that life has thrown at you.

It's hard to take a step back,
breathe, and reassess,
for what's been thrown upon you
has stolen your happiness.

For when you lose a happy face,
it takes a while to chill.
The pleasantries, the real life you
can't show your true goodwill.

I implore you to hand it over,
give your anger to our God.
Seek solace in the faith you have.
Let your honor not be flawed.

GUILTY

The cold blue steel of prison bars
left shadows in my cell.
Engulfed in this wretched place,
my life condemned to hell.

With the verdict read, the gavel dropped,
I found myself aghast,
that the model citizen I tried to be
was lost back in the past.

I never was a man to drink.
I loved my family.
Never knew the rage I felt
for a predator that came to be.

Represented as a friend,
a welcomed man was he.
Conversation for the wife,
well read and liked you see.

Until that day he stole her,
broke the family and the trust!
Destroyed the bond of matrimony
which ended with disgust.

With children devastated,
a world collapsed inside.
I couldn't bear the feeling.
He deceived and took my bride.

There never really was much thought
as I approached him with that gun.
Blew a hole right through him
before I turned to run.

Why?… I have no answer
for the rage placed in my sea.
In him, I saw the Devil
sent to torment me.

This door has closed and sealed my fate
for a life that I have led.
The jury had more compassion
for the man my wife had bed.

BODY, SOUL,& SPIRIT

Within each of us lies a spirit.
Instilled by our Creator.
Each must consider bonding with it
between the now and later.

Each day our body grows,
becomes the person we shall be.
The soul gaining wisdom
through the senses granted thee.

You see, the soul makes our decisions
reflects what the eyes can see.
Becomes the who in you
it's your personality.

We all live this life
in body and in soul,
ultimately departing,
some never reach the goal.

For spirit is the final stage
of the three parts of your being.
For in the body and the soul
lies the core the Lord is seeing.

The destination of the spirit
is mapped by how you live.
Becoming one with spirit
your sins the Lord forgives.

So when your time is finished
here upon the Earth,
body and soul remains,
your spirits gains rebirth.

BLESSED

You are blessed to be in America
where you can live in peace,
Blessed to reside in a country
and not live in Middle-East.

Israel is now filled with trauma
attacked by those with no moral clarity.
Chaos, mayhem, and death
has befallen on God's country.

Take heed my faithful followers,
this just might happen to us.
Our border is wide open
with a government we can't trust.

Our debt is overwhelming,
still we give to keep those free.
At risk are all our children
and a future with no guarantee.

Beside the mounting pressure
and the burdens we all share,
I ask you to take a moment
and show others that you care.

Hold a door, buy a meal
give up your place in line.
Little things will give you pride,
continued blessing you will find.

REMEMBERING D DAY

The clouds did part this D-day back in 1944
When I lay upon the blood-soaked sands,
and God opened up a door.

I saw a set of stairsteps
then peace came over me.
Should I not survive the battle,
there's a future I can see.

Bursting shells and flashing bullets.
Chaos amongst the men.
Working through the carnage,
we attacked again and again.

And when that bullet struck me
I gasped with painful breath,
then saw myself with others
who did not pass this test.

All gathered around the staircase
and linked up hand in hand.
Ascending to eternity
to the sound of an Angelic band.

BATTLEFIELD NOW GREEN

The cannons no longer rumble.
Smoke's cleared from the air.
Soldiers been forgotten
in an era of much despair.

Growing pains of a mighty nation
required a needed change.
Society could no longer accept the fact that
humans were bound in chains.

This division in the country
erupted in a Civil War.
600,000 lives were claimed.
Loved ones lost for evermore.

Evil was defeated.
God's glory finally seen.
That all men are created equal
and our grass can now grow green.

RESET FAST APPROACHING

Justice has been questioned
in a country with all men free.
A nation is being destroyed.
Increasing crime and anarchy.

Our eyes are open to it
and with despair we cannot see,
the Armies of Heaven's angels
preparing to set the Eagle free.

It may look like our rights are lost.
Be assured our house will stand.
These are words you need to hear
all across the land.

The wicked will be overthrown.
Justice will come soon.
Armies are amassing hold
faith for this great typhoon.

QUESTIONS

Can I cast a vote
without fear of manipulation?
Can I cast a vote
to keep free a great nation?

Can I vote free of corruption
amidst transparency and accountability?
Can I be assured again
and trust democracy?

Can I ever walk the streets
without fear pounding in my heart?
Can I know that my children
will not be stolen in the dark?

Can I have a little privacy
and safety in my home?
Can I rest assured that justice
is equal everywhere I roam?

Can I? Would I? Should I?
Questions fill my mind.
Can stars and stripes pass the test
facing all mankind.

Retirement

Lord's blessed me with this cabin
with a pool up in the woods.
Nature surrounding me,
free to relive my childhood.

Communing with His creation,
I view His tall pine trees,
catch glimpses of His greatness
in cascading waters before falls freeze.

He blesses me with sunshine,
and moonlit starry nights.
Warms my soul in fireside chats
beneath the northern lights.

Food, there is plenty.
There are no wants or needs.
I reside in God's creation,
having fulfilled my Earthly deeds.

SEEKING PERFECTION

Nothing's perfect in this world
though you might find it in a flower.
You might find it in a snowflake
but you'll look for hours and hours.

Perfections to be worked on
by all who walk the land.
Checking where you are in life
while God holds you in his hand.

You'll work to be a Christian
in honor and in deed.
You'll work to provide for family
for all their wants and needs.

Will you become perfect
while on this planet Earth?
A challenge to be worked on
since your blessed birth.

In reality we're all sinners.
It's just the world we're in.
Often tempted by Satin
and his demons in the wind.

Perfections on the other side
of this dimension in which we live.
Working to become one with it
blends the passage He will give.

Q& A

Between the questions and the answers
is the life that we all live,
seeking wise decision
with all we have to give.

Character and work ethic
continued learning as we go,
becoming wiser to our environment,
befriending people we've come to know.

Family is foundation.
Growth is what we need.
Reaching our destination
life's wounds are now remedied.

Many questions answered,
many answers still sought out.
We'll never settle all of them
and some will leave some doubt.

In the end, it just won't matter
as we reach our final day.
We'll reminisce the life we've lived,
unanswered questions fade away.

ERASING SHADOWS

Between the shadows and the substance
obscurity resides,
leaving souls quite restless,
destroying our earthly ride.

To live a life with substance
is something for which to stride.
Languishing in procrastination
is just a place to hide.

Step out of the shadows
and seek your destiny,
For God placed you on this Earth
and with you, He will always be.

Simply pray the question,
"What do you wish of me today?"
Believe your life has purpose
and continue on your way.

When your day has ended
stand tall without a crutch,
For shadows cannot linger
when there is substance in your touch.

ALWAYS NEAR

I know you have a partner
who you have loved for several years.
I know you have three children
Over which you have shed so many tears.

I know when your heart's heavy
and when you need some rest,
I've sat with you through hard times
and when you were at your best.

I've given you my lifetime,
twelve years been by your side.
Never growled in anger
even when you've hurt my pride.

Your table scraps haven't often been the best
but I never let you know.
Always looked up to you
with my little puppy glow.

I feel my end is nearing
and worry about you so,
Knowing this will cause you pain
and you will lose your smiling glow.

The only way to thank you
is the wagging of my tail.
Even now I find it hard to do
as I'm getting very frail.

I've given you my lifetime,
I wouldn't change a thing.
I've left a paw print in your heart
to ease my parting sting.

MOVING FORWARD

God's given you the strength.
It takes the inner will
to rise from the destruction,
your future to fulfill.

Don't tell me you can't do it.
Don't sit there without a smile.
The world is reaching out to you,
new life is not futile.

A family sees the worth in you.
They will never walk away.
Hear their words and act on them,
don't let fear stand in your way.

It might be one step forward
and then two steps to the rear.
Time and faith will heal all wounds
with success the Angel's cheer.

Nature's Gift

Captured on a park bench
sitting by the sea,
I realized the great beaut
in what God's presented me.

It's here I sit to reflect on life,
the paths that have been forsaken.
The heartaches and many sorrows
of decisions wrongly taken.

Communing with Mother Nature,
I see the need for this.
Pausing in the race of life
to grasp the blessings of His kiss.

Clouds obscure a future's sky
and the dawn yields to another day.
Serenity on a moonlit night
erases life's disarray.

WINGED RESCUE

I felt him by my bedside
my final married night.
Black eyes looking down upon me,
a steed of winged flight.

Mercurior was at my side
to take me from this space,
Fly me to another world
another dimension to embrace.

Tonight I did not call him.
He felt the need in me,
to save me from drowning
in tears of broken matrimony.

Tomorrow I sign the form
that means a certain death,
eighteen years of wedlock
being put to a final test.

How could this steed of satin white
sense the pain I feel,
find his way to be with me.
Is this a dream or is it real?

We exit through the sliding glass
and fly off in the night.
Starlit kisses cross my face,
I hold the mane so tight.

With words he speaks of better times
beyond this darkened sea.
This steed has come from up above,
he's here to rescue me.

From his saddle, I see the future.
We have ridden through the past.
I see there is a place for me
as I view the celestial mass.

And now back on my pillow
Mercurior exits into the night.
In search of weary haggard souls
to offer them a flight.

Tomorrow's a new beginning.
A contract I will sign.
Closing out the past
so the future I can find.

MY CHILD

On sullen nights alone and cold.
I find you sitting growing old.

In the warmth of fireside embers
I see you cry of things remembered.

I trust you heal from the pangs of past,
knowing tears may forever last.

Remember this those who are in this space
that I have put you in this race.

Be still and listen, for it's then you'll hear,
my love and my presence is always very near.

I continue standing at your door....
Why you have never heard the knock.

COURTYARD MYSTIQUE

Candles flicker in the courtyard
as I await the rise of a celestial moon.
Attuned to the reeded sounds of woodwinds,
it will be dark very soon.

Each night the spirits walk the path
of streets laid long ago.
This storied town of New Orleans
is a love I've come to know.

Three hundred years of history
along the Mississippi's path.
Stories of those who have lived and died,
many spirits have amassed.

Each night I see the shadow
along that aged brick wall,
and reach out into the past
envisioned lives and stories I recall.

I think they will never leave this town
of echoed music through the street,
bonding with French Quarter gas lights
till dawn brings their retreat.

CAUGHT IN A MOMENT

Have you ever found yourself
between the pages of birth and death,
sitting alone quite aimlessly
in vain your actions rendered.

You care not to look forward.
Your past, a door not opened.
Stagnant in the moment,
all energy of life now broken.

The calmness overwhelming,
the mind is caught in a trap.
You feel the sullen silence
yet in the moment you just snap back.

Where were you in that moment?
What made you pause your life?
A hiccup in a place called time
freed from world's stress and strife.

BROKEN

The future I was to have with you
now lost for evermore.
Photographic memories
never to be developed like before.

I'll view the moments of our past
and dream of times gone by.
My heart will heal from emptiness.
With time I will survive.

Our souls will cross on moonlit nights
and times when I'm all alone.
This gift of love now dormant,
windswept from the seeds I've sewn.

The future will bear new love,
new times will grace my path.
Acceptance of a grand new life,
never achievable without what's past.

HABERDASHERY

The days of haberdashery
are many years long past.
The ladies of the era
exuded so much class.

From Victorian belles to Art Deco,
ladies would stand out
To capture eyes of well-dressed men
with ruffles, furs, and lace to flout.

Today it's faded memories
that time of elegant grace,
The beauty of a lady
God gave us to embrace.

I AM THE STORM

Stand tall against the storm.
You were put here for a reason.
Let your light shine out upon the masses
excel through your accretion.

Take pride in your achievements,
keep your back against the wall.
Know that standing steadfast
is a deterrent against what may befall.

LEAVING PORT

I climb the masted riggings
win preparation for the sail.
Leaving family, friends, and possessions
in search of a holy grail.

We'll venture forth from harbored port
and travel tepid seas.
Moving with Mother Nature,
entrusting the summer breeze.

There are islands to discover.
Societies yet unseen.
Treasures may await us
it's just a dream.

Sun breaks on distant horizon.
The men are all aboard.
Casks of rum and vitals
safely have been stored.

And now we drop the main sail.
The jib is all intact.
We're off to sail the mighty sea,
never knowing if we'll be back.

STILL WITH YOU

My light will shine upon you
each and every day,
guiding you along your path
in a life of disarray.

Today I send you sunbeams,
in shadows I hold your hand.
Awaiting your arrival
celebrations I have planned.

On cloudy days I walk with you,
I sit by your bedside late at night.
Each day I hold you in my arms
and help you fight life's fight.

Know that I am with you
in photos that you see.
I'll shine my light upon you
and guide you through a stormy sea.

SUNDAY'S STRENGTH

Another week has come and gone.
I see no change in me.
I've weathered through the snow and ice
and face a brand-new week.

I face another bill to pay,
many chores are left undone.
And when I look at society,
I see I'm not the only one.

Tomorrow starts another day,
I'll seek the Lord's loving grace.
Place myself in His arms
and the holiness of His place.

It's there in dreams I'll gain some strength
to survive this earthly bleed,
commune with all the followers,
find wisdom in the word indeed.

Then I will place it all beneath my cap
having shaken hands and left,
and begin my walk another week
with faith and direction set.

AGE AND WISDOM

Birthdays come and birthdays go
as the seasons pass with time.
Each adds a little wisdom
with direction we align.

For some, it takes a bit longer,
others find it fast.
The reason for our being
and why our souls were cast.

Our purpose overshadowed
by societal demands.
Busy in the workplace,
no time to place our hands.

Through life, we'll touch another.
Perhaps not meaning so.
Your drink will fall upon the lips
of one you might not know.

That's why you build your character
and live your life with grace.
It just might be your purpose
to put a smile on another's face.

VALENTINE

If I had not met you,
I know not where I'd be.
Life would be much different
had I traveled a tormented sea.

My children would have different lives,
less smiles and needed words.
Encouragement and direction
lifting precious lives upwards.

Today you are my Valentine,
a word I can't define.
Knowing that without you
two souls could not have aligned.

Know that I am with you
though a thousand miles away.
I am your forever Valentine
awaiting our next matinee.

DECISIONS

Would you travel to the moon and back
for the one you love so dear.
Knowing the road is not guaranteed
and its path not very clear?

Would you travel to the moon and back
assured you have the fuel?
Would you chance the fate of being stranded
in a journey that could be so cruel?

Would you risk it all, begin the trip
without the needed tools,
to rescue you along your way
stranded with other noted fools?

Take time and prepare your journey
Know the route to take.
Cutting corners in love's embrace
could lead to an awful fate.

STARRY NIGHTS

Fireflies flash amongst the trees,
crickets chirp each night.
Aside the crackling fire pit
I marvel with delight.

Pine tips point toward twinkling stars
and in constellations I do see,
a zodiac's interpretation
of those surrounding me.

So much mystery in the universe,
"the when", "the why", "the where".
On starlit nights I take the time
to sit alone and stare.

It's here I find reflection
and answers so often sought.
Commune with our creator
immersed in deeper thought.

ANCHORED

Delivered to a rest home
at the age of eighty-three,
I find myself in quiet reminisce,
of what life has dealt to me.

Staring out the window
as twilight touches the bay.
I realize the wind blows through my sails
and I struggle to stay afloat each day.

Life's adventure has been exciting,
many stories to be told.
Now I'm put to anchor
with others growing old.

I'll sail the seas in restless dreams,
feel the brine mist on my face.
Relive the joys of youthfulness,
escaping this dreadful place.

GREAT RACE OF 1870

The era of the steamboat
is nostalgia of the past.
Majestic in their presence,
an era that could not last.

Travelers found their passage
from St Louis to New Orleans.
Farmers moved their produce
on these floating great machines.

One hundred fifty years ago
two steamers had a race.
Big Easy the destination
who would take first place.

Robert E Lee and the Natchez
churned the Mississip.
Boilers stoked with firewood
for this historic trip.

The Lee would take the checkered
and for sixteen years she sailed,
till finally meeting its' demise
with fire in the cotton baled.

SEASIDE

If I could have a little house
tucked along Narraganset Bay,
I would find myself in peaceful bliss
each and every day.

From sunrise to sunset
warmth would be upon my skin,
and in times of rainy weather
enjoy the raindrops on rooftops tin.

Seaside sounds and passing yachts
would catch my ear and eye,
for at this stage in a blessed life
I could just enjoy time go by.

PRISM OF LIFE

We live life in a prism
where each day we have a glow.
Somedays bright and shiny,
Others we just don't know.

In reds, we see the love we share.
Greens, our growing worth.
Blues and darkened colors
are sometimes sadness here on Earth.

The oranges and the yellows
mix with the lighting from above.
Within this prism that we live
is the beauty often lost sight of.

This light show's ever-present
in this world in which we reside.
We're blessed to experience all colors
from God's prism's faceted side.

TIME

There's one thing that we need
but is impossible to find.
You can search through out your whole life,
it's the passage of time.

It's the one thing you can't buy
that we all could use each day.
Just a little more time
to calm the disarray.

An extra cup of coffee,
time to just relax.
Enjoy that little cat nap
to help fill life's widening cracks.

We never have enough
and more we cannot get.
In every demographic
time is forever set.

WALK OF LIFE

Today I took my grandson
for a walk down memory lane,
telling him great stories
of trucks and planes and trains.

I told him of my childhood
and all the games I played.
Sat upon the park side bench,
njoyed a lemonade.

We spoke of God and parents
and answered many "Whys".
He starred at me intently
with tender loving eyes.

It was then I knew we bonded.
My time growing so very short
to fill his tank with knowledge
and entrust my whole support.

My life now filled with wisdom.
With love it flowed from me
to nurture this growing youth
into the man I'd like to see.

BEST OF TIMES

Classic cars and pin-ups
just to live there once again.
Chatting on the porch swing
enjoying iced tea with my friends.

Looking back I see the 50s,
the 60s and so much more,
all that great home cooking
that mother had in store.

Couldn't wait to leave the house
at five or even sooner.
Independence in the family car
with AM music on the tuner.

That early rock n roll
turned into a classic soul.
Necking at the drive-in,
better morals kept us in control.

There were no guns just fistfights.
Rivals all around.
Couldn't wait for Friday night
when football sparked the town.

Then a graduation,
a break from first girlfriend.
In dreams, I relive all the moments
knowing now it's just pretend.

For those who read this special piece,
know that your past you'll reminisce,
and the one thing you will never forget
was the joy of first teenage kiss.

CAR CRUISE CONNECTION

Classic cars and a buffed old man
caught my eye this day.
50s music in the background,
I knew I had to stay.

That 57 T bird really caught my eye.
The stately well-dressed gentleman
winked as I walked by.

In casual conversation
we spoke of this and that,
getting to know some basics
with some humor in the chat.

He told me of his prom night,
this car, and about the town,
the sweetheart he once married,
a life of ups and downs.

And as I sought to just move on,
he reached out for my hand.
Asked why such a beauty
had no wedding band.

I told him the tragic ending
of a love that could never last.
He suggested coffee and a cruise,
top-down would be a blast.

We hit it off that summer's night.
Oldies filled the air.
And now I own a T-bird
to go with my long blonde hair.

UFO's

The land of the midnight sun
is known for the aurora light.
Many are unaware mysteries abound
on any given night.

Citizens are quite troubled
by sightings in the late-night sky.
UFOs, they call them.
There are questions of what and why.

Over several decades
sixteen thousand will disappear.
The Alaskan triangle has claimed these lives,
people walk the nights in fear.

Lights in formation.
No sounds the crafts do make.
Disappearing in a flash,
these visions are not fake.

Yes, there are many questions
looking into celestial stars,
so when we look up to the universe
know there may be men from Mars.

BOOKS

The greatest gift one can receive
is the knowledge from a book.
Immerse yourself in an author's brush
and let him set the hook.

Knowledge is the key to life
in books, you'll learn to see.
Each book will hold a special place
in your mental cavity.

So fill your head with printed text.
Your life will be much brighter.
Take the time to align yourself
with the one known as the writer.

POET'S UNIVERSE

The vastness of thought
and the concept of space and time,
bring this gifted poet
endless writes to rhyme.

What is this mantra
where words fit in between,
the thought and time continuum
where things just can't be seen?

Today it's patriotic,
tomorrow life of pain.
I find a little humor
and write about the rain.

I see fire on the mountain
burning candles in the night,
vision, moonbeams in a bottle,
and creatures out of sight.

I feel great writers calling
for me to produce a profound piece.
So mentally I find the space
to pen what thought and time release.

Thank You Jerrel Wolfe

www.ingramcontent.com/pod-product-compliance
Lightning Source LLC
Chambersburg PA
CBHW051220120626
46547CB00013B/1436